Tips to Achieve Great Things

The Unexpected Elements That Determine Every Project's End

by

Brian J. Coffey

Table of Contents

Introduction

Projects, great or little, are at the foundation of human growth and development. From modest house modifications to space exploration expeditions, they impact our everyday lives and push the frontiers of what is possible. However, the success or failure of any project is not simply decided by its scale or complexity. In truth, there are numerous unforeseen aspects that might ultimately influence the destiny of a project.

This revolutionary book digs into the inner workings of project management and unveils the crucial aspects that may make or ruin a project. It gives useful insights and practical solutions for project success.

One of the primary aspects that affect the outcome of a project is the human element. Despite the developments in technology and equipment, projects are ultimately carried out by people. Their talents, motivation, and communication play a key part in the result of every project. Smith analyzes how understanding and efficiently managing human dynamics may dramatically affect the outcome of a project.

Another surprise variable that might impact a project's outcome is culture. Each project is immersed in a distinct cultural environment, and failing to realize and negotiate these cultural variations may lead to misunderstandings, delays, and even failure. Smith digs into the complexity of cultural relations and presents practical methods for addressing these problems.

In addition to the psychological and cultural aspects, there are other extrinsic components that might impact a project's result. These might vary from economic developments and political changes to natural calamities and unforeseen occurrences. We will examine how to anticipate and minimize these external issues to keep a project on schedule.

This book goes beyond typical project management practices and analyzes the importance of creativity, innovation, and risk-taking in project success. It highlights how thinking outside the box and accepting calculated risks may lead to new results and push the limits of what is possible.

Through real-life examples and fascinating tales, we deliver a thorough and practical guide for project managers, team leaders, and everyone engaged in bringing huge initiatives to a conclusion. It challenges conventional concepts of project management and gives a unique viewpoint on how to handle the complexity of every project, regardless of its size or scope.

This is a necessary read for anybody trying to grasp the underlying aspects that decide the outcome of a project. It delivers useful insights, practical solutions, and thought-provoking debates that will revolutionize the way we approach and execute projects. Whether you're a project manager, a team member, or just interested in the inner workings of successful projects, this book will be an eye-opening and instructive read.

Chapter One

Vision and Planning

In the realm of project management, the route to success starts with a clear and appealing goal and a well-thought-out strategy to accomplish it. Vision and planning are the core aspects that set the scene for any project, whether it's a simple house improvement or a major space exploration effort.

The Power of Clear Vision in Project Initiatives

In the area of project management, a clear and compelling vision acts as the North Star that directs all efforts and choices. Whether you're starting on a small-scale home remodel or coordinating a huge space exploration expedition, the power of your project's vision may make the difference between success and failure.

Defining a Compelling Project Vision

A project's vision is like a beacon of light that lights the route ahead. It encompasses the overall aim, the intended end-state, and the values that drive the project. But what makes a project vision compelling?

- Clarity: A captivating vision is crystal clear, leaving no opportunity for ambiguity. It offers a clear image of what success looks like and ensures that everyone engaged knows the project's ultimate purpose.

- Inspiration: A compelling vision doesn't only enlighten; it inspires. It stirs the emotions and passions of the team, fuelling their devotion to the project's achievement.

- Alignment: The vision links all stakeholders towards a single aim. It integrates the team's activities, creating cooperation and synergy.

- Longevity: A vision should endure the test of time. It stays relevant even as the project progresses, acting as a consistent reference point.

Communicating the Vision to other Team Members and Stakeholders

Having a clear vision is one thing; successfully expressing it is another. Without efficient communication, a great concept might stay dormant or get lost in translation. To ensure your project's vision is understood and accepted, consider the following:

- Storytelling: Craft an engaging story that expresses the core of the concept.

Use tales and analogies to make the vision relevant and remembered.

- Inclusivity: Involve team members and stakeholders in the formulation and refining of the vision. When kids have a stake in developing it, they are more inclined to accept ownership

- Consistency: Reiterate the vision frequently. Whether it's via meetings, publications, or visual aids, repetition emphasizes the vision's value and ensures everyone stays on the same page.

- Visual Aids: Employ visual aids like diagrams, charts, and presentations to make the vision concrete. Visual aids help clarify complicated topics and boost understanding.

The Role of Vision in Motivating and Inspiring the Team

A fascinating vision is a great motivator. It fills the endeavor with a feeling of purpose and sparks the enthusiasm of everyone participating. Here's how vision inspires motivation:

- Meaningful Work: When team members understand the link between their jobs and the wider goal, their work takes on more significance. This feeling of purpose fuels motivation.

- Resilience: In the midst of obstacles, a clear vision functions as a source of resilience. It recalls the team why they began the project in the first place and inspires them to persist.

- Innovation: A well-defined vision may spark innovative thinking.

Team members are more inclined to explore imaginative solutions and push the limits of what's possible when they are united with a compelling vision.

A well-crafted vision is the cornerstone of each successful endeavor. It gives clarity, inspiration, and alignment, ensuring that all efforts are focused towards a shared purpose. When conveyed successfully, the vision has the capacity to excite and inspire the team, converting an ordinary project into an amazing one.

Chapter Two

Leadership and Team Dynamics

Effective leadership and harmonious team relations are the lifeblood of every project, whether it's a small-scale house remodel or a huge space exploration expedition. In this chapter, we will discuss the essential role that leadership plays in determining the project's direction and the synergy of team dynamics in driving it toward success.

The Role of Leadership in Project Execution

Leadership in project management is not simply about possessing a title; it's about directing the team with vision, honesty, and skill. Let's look into the important characteristics of leadership in project execution:

Setting the Vision and Direction

A successful leader sets and communicates the project's vision and goals, ensuring that every team member is on the same page. This vision not only offers purpose but also acts as a roadmap for the team.

Decision-Making and Problem-Solving

Effective leaders are proficient at making educated judgments rapidly. They also possess the problem-solving abilities essential to manage the inevitable problems and barriers that occur throughout a project.

Communication and Transparency

Open and open communication is a characteristic of successful leadership. Leaders must keep the team informed, listen to comments, and build a culture of trust and cooperation.

Delegation and Empowerment

Leadership entails delegating and enabling team members to take responsibility for their roles. This not only eases the leader's load but also enables the team to flourish.

Building High-Performing Teams

A project's success is not entirely reliant on the leader but also on the cohesiveness and effectiveness of the team. Let's study the components of developing high-performing teams:

Diversity and Inclusion

Diverse teams provide various views and skill sets, which may lead to more imaginative solutions. Inclusion guarantees that every team member's voice is heard and respected.

Team Roles and Responsibilities

Clearly defined roles and duties reduce overlap and misunderstanding. When each team member understands their function, tasks are completed more effectively.

Conflict Resolution and Collaboration

Conflicts are unavoidable, but how they are handled may make or destroy a project. Strong teams are proficient at resolving disagreements and working together amicably.

Motivation and Team Spirit

Motivated team members tend to be more productive and innovative. Effective leaders inspire and promote a feeling of camaraderie among team members.

Chapter Three

Effective Communication

Effective communication is a critical component in every project's success. It ensures that all team members are on the same page, working towards the same objectives, and aware of any possible problems or changes. The Surprising Factors That Determine the Fate of Every Project underscore the necessity of excellent communication in the success or failure of a project. Let us look into the different ways in which excellent communication plays a key part in deciding the destiny of a project.

Clear Understanding of Goals and Roles

One of the primary aspects that affect the success of a project is a clear knowledge of the project objectives and the roles and duties of each team member. Effective communication plays a critical part in ensuring that everyone is aware of their unique activities and how they contribute to the broader project goals. This knowledge allows team members to remain focused, motivated, and oriented towards the project's success. Regular communication and updates between team members also aid in spotting any possible misconceptions or overlaps in duties, ensuring that the project continues smoothly.

Efficient Problem-Solving

No endeavor is free from hurdles or issues. However, how these difficulties are managed may make or break a project's destiny. Effective communication is vital in addressing and resolving any difficulties that develop throughout the project.

It lets team members express their ideas, come up with unique solutions, and make educated choices. Regular communication also helps in recognizing possible difficulties early on, enabling the team to take proactive actions to avert any setbacks.

Building Trust and Collaboration

Trust and teamwork are important parts of a successful endeavor. Effective communication plays a critical role in creating and sustaining trust among team members. When team members are upfront and open in their communication, it generates a healthy and collaborative work atmosphere. This, in turn, leads to greater cooperation, higher production, and ultimately, a successful project.

Managing Changes and Adaptability

In today's fast-paced corporate world, projects are prone to changes in timetables, budgets, and scope. Effective communication is vital in handling these changes and ensuring that they do not derail the project's progress. With open and honest communication, team members may debate and understand the reasons behind the changes and adjust appropriately. This not only assists in keeping the project on schedule but also enhances team members' capacity to manage unanticipated obstacles in the future.

Effective Resource Management

Projects depend on many resources, including time, money, and personnel. Effective communication plays a critical role in managing these resources properly.

When team members communicate consistently and effectively, it assists in recognizing possible resource restrictions early on, allowing for necessary modifications to be made. This assists in preventing any delays or setbacks and keeps the project on track toward its ultimate conclusion.

Managing Stakeholder Expectations

Stakeholders play a key role in a project's success. They have certain expectations and standards that need to be satisfied. Effective communication is vital in managing these expectations and keeping stakeholders informed about the project's progress. By keeping stakeholders connected and engaged, team members may ensure that the project fits with their expectations, leading to overall project success.

Effective communication is a critical instrument in deciding the destiny of a project. From the earliest planning phases until the project's conclusion, continuous and clear communication among team members and stakeholders is vital. It promotes a clear knowledge of objectives and responsibilities, efficient problem-solving, trust and cooperation, flexibility to change, effective resource management, and managing stakeholder expectations. Projects that emphasize good communication are more likely to succeed, fulfill stakeholders' expectations, and achieve the targeted goals. In today's corporate environment, where projects are getting more complicated and time-sensitive, efficient communication is no longer only a beneficial tool but a vital one for project success.

Chapter Four

Managing Risk and Uncertainty

Risk and unpredictability are two terms that project managers are all too acquainted with. In each project – no matter the size or scope – there are always aspects of risk and uncertainty that might impact its result. These issues may originate from both external and internal sources, making it vital for project managers to have methods in place to handle them successfully.

Managing risk and uncertainty is a technique that is vital for the success of every endeavor. It entails identifying possible risks and uncertainties, considering their potential influence on the project, and applying solutions to reduce their consequences.

This tool is particularly essential in the context of "The Surprising Factors That Determine the Fate of Every Project" because it helps project managers proactively address possible concerns and avert project failure.

The first step in managing risk and uncertainty as a tool is to identify possible risks and uncertainties. This requires doing a complete evaluation of the project, including the scope, timeframe, resources, and parties involved. Project managers must also evaluate external issues, such as market trends, economic circumstances, and political events that might affect the project.

Once possible risks and uncertainties have been identified, the following stage is to examine their potential effect on the project.

This entails analyzing the probability of the hazards happening and the possible repercussions if they do. It is crucial for project managers to prioritize risks depending on their severity since this will help them identify which hazards demand urgent attention and which can be monitored and managed over time.

After identifying and assessing possible risks and uncertainties, project managers must establish measures to minimize their influence on the project. These tactics might include risk minimization, risk transfer, risk avoidance, and risk acceptance. Risk mitigation entails making proactive efforts to lessen the possibility or effect of a risk. This might involve contingency planning, establishing safety precautions, or building backup plans.

Risk transfer entails moving the burden of the risk to another party via contracts, insurance, or outsourcing. Risk avoidance entails totally removing the risk by avoiding the activity or event that might lead to it. Finally, risk acceptance entails understanding the risk and its possible effects, but opting to continue with the undertaking regardless.

In addition to controlling risks and uncertainties, it is also vital for project managers to communicate and cooperate with stakeholders throughout the project. This involves keeping them informed about possible risks and uncertainties and including them in the decision-making process. By incorporating stakeholders, project managers may acquire useful insights and viewpoints, which can assist in identifying and managing possible risks and uncertainties.

Lastly, it is vital to monitor and analyze risks and uncertainties during the life of the project. As projects mature, new risks and uncertainties may arise, and existing ones may vary in severity or probability. By continually monitoring and analyzing risks, project managers may adapt and apply new techniques to manage them efficiently.

Managing risk and uncertainty is a vital component in the success of any endeavor. By recognizing possible risks and uncertainties, understanding their impact, and applying proactive methods, project managers may successfully manage these elements and raise the odds of project success. Additionally, continual communication and engagement with stakeholders, as well as frequent monitoring and evaluation of risks, are critical for efficiently managing risks and uncertainties throughout the project's lifespan. With effective use of this technology, project managers can negotiate the unexpected nature of projects and ensure their successful conclusion.

Chapter Five

Resource Allocation and Management

Resource allocation and management is a critical instrument in guaranteeing the success of any project. It is the process of identifying, organizing, and managing diverse resources such as people, time, and materials to fulfill project goals efficiently and effectively. The Surprising Factors That Determine the Fate of Every Project underscores the notion that resource allocation and management a crucial component in determining the success or failure of a project.

One of the most critical components in resource allocation and management is determining the needed resources for a project. This comprises human resources, such as project managers, team members, and stakeholders, as well as physical resources like equipment, facilities, and supplies. It is vital to have a solid grasp of the project scope and goals to appropriately identify the required resources.

Once the resources have been identified, the following step is to distribute them properly. This entails allocating duties and tasks to team members depending on their skill sets and availability. It is crucial to ensure that resources are distributed in a manner that maximizes their usage and prevents any bottlenecks or overlaps. For instance, allocating a job to a team member who does not have the requisite expertise might lead to delays and damage the entire project timeframe.

Effective resource management also requires setting a realistic project timeline.

This involves evaluating the time and effort necessary for each activity and allocating resources appropriately. A thorough timetable might aid in recognizing possible challenges and changing the resource allocation as required. It is vital to remember that resource allocation is a dynamic process and may need to be altered during the project to guarantee its success.

Another key part of resource management is monitoring and tracking the consumption of resources. This may be done by frequent updates and progress reports from team members, as well as through project management tools and software. It is crucial to have a system in place to identify and handle any resource restrictions or conflicts in a timely way.

This may avoid bottlenecks and delays and keep the project on schedule.

Resource allocation and management also entail excellent communication with all parties engaged in the project. This involves keeping them informed about progress, any changes in resource allocation, and any possible concerns that may harm the project. Effective communication may assist in eliminating miscommunications and ensure that all team members are on the same page, working towards the same objective.

The Surprising Factors That Determine the Fate of Every Project highlights that resource allocation and management is not only about assigning tasks and measuring progress. It is also about knowing the capabilities and constraints of resources and making strategic choices to guarantee their optimal exploitation. It entails striking a balance between the project's scope, goals, and available resources.

Resource allocation and management an important element in project management, and their efficacy may influence the destiny of a project. It entails finding, arranging, and managing resources in a manner that maximizes their usage and assures project success. A full knowledge of the project and its resources, excellent communication, and ongoing monitoring are critical aspects of successful resource allocation and management.

Chapter Six

Handling Change and Adaptability

Handling change and adaptation are crucial skills that influence the outcome of any endeavor. In today's fast-paced and ever-changing business environment, initiatives encounter a plethora of unforeseen circumstances that may greatly affect their performance. These unexpected components might occur in the shape of new technology, changes in market trends, changed stakeholder agendas, or unplanned external events. Therefore, it is vital for each project to be prepared with efficient methods and approaches to manage change and flexibility in order to effectively navigate through these unforeseen components.

Change is inevitable in every undertaking. No matter how meticulously planned and performed a project is, it is guaranteed to meet unforeseen factors. These might emerge from internal sources such as evolving customer needs or external ones like changes in rules or economic situations. The capacity to manage change successfully is vital as it guarantees that a project can remain on track and produce its targeted goals. Similarly, flexibility is another key characteristic of project management that allows a project to react to unforeseen aspects in a flexible and proactive way. It entails the willingness to accept change and make required modifications to achieve project success.

A crucial part of managing change and flexibility is a proactive mentality.

This involves having the capacity to foresee probable changes and having a flexible strategy in place to handle them. It also includes having a team that is open to change and ready to continually adapt and modify to meet new situations. This mentality enables a project to keep ahead of any unforeseen components and proactively handle them before they create severe interruptions.

Handling change and flexibility also involves efficient communication and stakeholder management. As unexpected components might affect numerous facets of a project, it is vital to keep all stakeholders informed and aligned with any adjustments. This provides openness and creates confidence among team members and stakeholders, lowering the possibility of conflict and resistance to change.

Along with communication, having a robust and adaptable project team is crucial in managing change and flexibility. A team that is open to acquiring new skills, methods, and procedures can swiftly react to unexpected factors and discover inventive solutions to new issues. A varied team with various views and experiences may bring new ideas to the table and help to make solid judgments when encountering unexpected aspects.

Furthermore, having a solid change management strategy in place is vital for efficiently addressing change and flexibility. This comprises a methodical strategy for managing changes, including analyzing their effects, communicating effectively, and executing them in an orderly and controlled way.

The change management process should also comprise frequent reviews and updates to verify that modifications are aligned with the project's goals and objectives.

Handling change and adaptation are crucial capabilities in navigating through unforeseen aspects that might affect the outcome of a project. It takes a proactive approach, good communication, a resilient and adaptable staff, and a well-structured change management strategy. Projects that can successfully manage change and adapt to changing conditions are more likely to succeed and achieve their targeted results. Therefore, project managers must prioritize creating and executing methods to handle change and flexibility in order to maximize their chances of success in today's ever-changing corporate environment.

Chapter Seven

Corporate Endeavors: Navigating Business Projects

Corporate projects are activities done inside a firm or organization, which might vary from introducing new goods, expanding into new markets, reorganizing operations, or making strategic changes. These projects tend to be more complicated and diverse than smaller-scale initiatives, such as house improvements. Here's an explanation of the important topics and tactics mentioned in the chapter:

1. Complexity of Corporate Projects:

- Multifaceted Stakeholder Engagement: Corporate initiatives often engage a broad spectrum of stakeholders. This includes executives, workers, consumers, investors, regulatory agencies, and more.

Effective involvement and alignment among these varied groups are vital. Ensuring sure everyone knows the project's aims and is dedicated to its success is a task in itself.

- Market Dynamics and rivalry: Business initiatives are typically impacted by quickly changing market circumstances and severe rivalry. This dynamic economy needs adaptation and a thorough awareness of industry trends and rivals.

- Financial ramifications: Corporate initiatives may have considerable financial ramifications. This comprises managing finances, receiving funds, and ensuring that the project achieves a return on investment (ROI). Financial factors are essential concerns in company undertakings.

- Long-Term Strategy: Corporate initiatives are often related to an organization's long-term strategic goals. This implies there must be a clear relationship between the project's aims and the overall vision of the business. Ensuring that the project promotes the strategic direction of the firm is crucial.

2. Strategies for Navigating Business Projects:

- Strategic Alignment: The first step in managing corporate initiatives is ensuring that they fit with the organization's overarching strategy and objectives. This alignment gives a clear sense of purpose, ensuring that the project contributes to the company's vision and objectives.

- Effective Leadership: Strong leadership is vital in business initiatives.

Leaders must possess the ability to motivate and manage their teams, make difficult choices, and keep stakeholders informed. They need to negotiate the complexity of the corporate world.

- Risk Management: Corporate initiatives generally come with increased risks owing to their magnitude and possible financial repercussions. Effective risk management methods are critical for recognizing, analyzing, and mitigating any obstacles that might endanger the project's success.

- Change Management: Business initiatives typically need changes in procedures, structures, and systems. Effective change management is important to guarantee a seamless transition and the effective acceptance of these changes by workers and other stakeholders.

- Performance Measurement: To monitor the progress and assess the effect of business initiatives, key performance indicators (KPIs) are defined. Regular performance evaluations aid in making informed choices and required modifications to keep the project on track and aligned with the organization's objectives.

Chapter Eight

Space Exploration and Beyond: The Pinnacle of Project Management

Space exploration is a discipline that represents the height of human aspiration and scientific accomplishment. It entails launching expeditions to examine faraway planets, moons, asteroids, and even the extreme edges of our cosmos. These initiatives are highly difficult and need a degree of project management competence that is unsurpassed. Here's a more extensive explanation of the important topics and thoughts covered in this chapter:

1. The Challenges of Space Exploration:

- Vast Distances and Unpredictable Environments: Space missions must contend with the enormity of the universe.

The distances involved are huge, and the conditions are sometimes unexpected and dangerous. Spacecraft and missions confront high temperatures, radiation, microgravity, and the vacuum of space. Navigating and living under such circumstances is a massive task.

- Technological Complexity: The technology necessary for space travel is at the cutting edge of human understanding. Spacecraft, rovers, and research equipment are extremely specialized and need extraordinary engineering and ingenuity. Developing, testing, and deploying these systems involves knowledge in a broad variety of scientific and technical fields.

- Stringent Safety and Reliability: Safety is crucial in space exploration. Failures may have disastrous effects.

As a consequence, space programs emphasize durability and redundancy in equipment and systems. Rigorous testing and quality control are necessary to reduce the dangers associated with these complicated missions.

- International Collaboration: Space exploration frequently entails collaboration among numerous nations and international space organizations. International cooperation brings together various parties with varied interests and aims. Effective coordination and collaboration are necessary to handle these big, multi-national projects effectively.

2. Lessons from Space Exploration

- Vision and Long-Term Devotion: Space endeavors, like sending rovers to Mars or launching space telescopes, need long-term vision and unshakable devotion.

They typically entail years or even decades of preparation, development, and implementation. These missions highlight the value of having a clear vision and the patience to pursue big, long-term goals.

- Precision and Attention to Detail: In space exploration, there is no room for mistakes. The success of missions hinges on accuracy and precise attention to detail. Even tiny missteps might lead to mission failure. Therefore, planning and execution must be exact and carefully quality-controlled.

- Risk Management and Contingency Planning: Space missions are vulnerable to a number of dangers, ranging from equipment failures to unanticipated astronomical phenomena. Rigorous risk management methods are necessary to detect, analyze, and minimize these risks.

Comprehensive contingency planning is necessary to guarantee that missions can adapt to unanticipated problems.

- Innovation and adaptation: Space exploration stimulates innovation and adaptation. The unique constraints of space missions frequently need imaginative problem-solving and the creation of breakthrough technology. Space initiatives push the frontiers of what is feasible in engineering and science.

- Global Collaboration and Diplomacy: Space exploration frequently includes collaboration among different governments. This underlines the need for effective global collaboration and diplomatic ties to accomplish common goals.

Space initiatives transcend national borders and need diplomacy to manage international agreements, data-sharing, and resource distribution.

In summary, The lessons acquired from space exploration are essential and may be applied to projects of all kinds, giving insights into managing complexity, pursuing ambitious objectives, and efficiently minimizing risk in numerous activities. It underlines the special character of space exploration and its role in pushing the frontiers of human knowledge and capacity.

Conclusion

We have begun an examination of the complicated world of project management, stretching from the relatively small boundaries of home renovations to the awe-inspiring domain of space exploration. What we've learned is that regardless of the magnitude or complexity of a project, there are universal concepts, difficulties, and lessons that drive the art and science of getting large things done.

Throughout this book, we've gone into a broad range of projects, each offering its particular set of problems and lessons. Home improvements have taught us about the value of a clear vision, flexibility, and the skill of managing small-scale initiatives. Corporate initiatives have uncovered the challenges of aligning projects with long-term strategy, the requirement for good leadership, and the crucial significance of risk management. And in the infinite expanse of space exploration, we've observed the ultimate difficulties of accuracy, vision, global cooperation, and invention.

What connects these varied initiatives together is the overall framework of project management. Project management is the discipline that gives structure, advice, and a methodical strategy to navigating the tumultuous seas of project execution. It's the compass that keeps initiatives on track, regardless of their size or the environment in which they operate.

From clear project vision and effective leadership to communication, risk management, and flexibility, the techniques and insights acquired from these disparate initiatives are universal.

They are not restricted to any single sector but may be used for undertakings in business, science, art, or any other effort where objectives need to be reached.

As you shut the book and begin on your own path of project management, remember that the destiny of every project, from the most modest to the most ambitious, lies in the hands of individuals who grasp the unexpected aspects that influence success. It is a combination of rigorous preparation, inspired leadership, effective communication, diligent risk management, and the capacity to react to the unexpected.

We hope that the information you've learned from this book will act as a compass on your own road to creating outstanding achievements.

The world is loaded with chances for greatness, and with the appropriate tools and mentality, you can negotiate the complexity of project management and make big things happen, whether it's a house remodel a business initiative, or even a trip to the stars.